LIFE LESSONS

REFLECTIONS ON THE ART OF TEACHING

ALBERT PERRY

authorHOUSE

1663 LIBERTY DRIVE, SUITE 200
BLOOMINGTON, INDIANA 47403
(800) 839-8640
www.authorhouse.com

First published by AuthorHouse 07/01/04

ISBN: 1-4184-0580-9 (e)
ISBN: 1-4184-0581-7 (sc)

Printed in the United States of America
Bloomington, Indiana

This book is printed on acid-free paper.

To those along the way who helped to teach me many of life's important lessons, both inside and outside of the classroom - students, parents, friends, relatives, and colleagues

ACKNOWLEDGMENTS

I would like to express my gratitude to two blue-ribbon educators who offered praise as well as constructive criticism in the early stages of the manuscript: Nick Thacher, formerly head of the New Canaan Country School for many years, and Don Eron, a longtime member of the English Department at the University of Colorado. And thanks also to my sister Ginger, in Boulder, and my niece Eden, both of whom were always quick to offer their unflagging support, in ways both spoken and unspoken.

"I have come to believe that a great teacher is a great artist and that there are as few as there are any other great artists. Teaching might even be the greatest of the arts since the medium is the mind and spirit."

John Steinbeck

Introduction

We all know the old saying, "Those that can, do. Those that can't, teach." These words typify a fairly common attitude that many people harbor when it comes to members of the teaching profession. The fact is that school teachers get a bad rap these days. It's a contradiction, too. As a society we all agree upon the need for better results in the classroom, but as individuals we tend to devalue those people who are active as teachers in the field of education.

So I'll state my case right here at the outset: Teaching is the most noble of all the arts. There is nothing in the world more creative, and more demanding, than capturing, and holding, the attention of a classroom full of students. If you don't believe me, you should try it some time.

Of course, you'll seldom hear teachers talking about their work in terms of an art form. Most people would say that a person has to be creating something in order to qualify as an artist. We all share the image of the lonely artist slaving away in obscurity in an effort to create a beautiful painting. People tend to think of creativity only in terms of art: painting a picture, writing a novel, or sculpting a statue. But I believe we need to view the subjects of art and creativity in an entirely different way.

It may be that the most creative people in life are those individuals who are able to channel their energies on a daily basis, at home or on the job, and in their relationships with other human beings. They are usually the kind of people who serve a higher purpose in life. That is, they usually think in terms of serving the needs of others. "How can I help?" becomes a more important question than "What's in it for me?" In this light, teaching really does become a kind of art form. As Henry David Thoreau wrote, "To affect the quality of the day, that is the highest of the arts." The fact is that teachers get to affect the quality of the lives of their students every single day.

As an English teacher, I have come to believe that living a good life is a lot more important than writing a great novel. In the first place, the writing of fiction is a solitary act which by its nature involves a process that tends to isolate rather than unify the spirit. The truth is that in their daily lives people need to have a communion with other human beings in order to satisfy many of their deepest and most basic needs. Secondly, those who create works of fiction very often use their writing as a way to come to terms with the painful aspects of their own past. It's obvious that artists seem to pay a higher price for their efforts. When you read the story of their lives, there's usually a lot of pain and suffering that goes along with a certain kind of creative energy. That's why so many writers of fiction speak about the *need* to create. Thomas Mann, the German novelist, spoke for the majority when he referred to "the artist's sublime *revenge* on his experience." But the problem is that the words of the novelist invariably fail to heal the pain because writing a novel only serves as a substitute for the real thing. It's the same for all of the creative arts, too, because in a very real sense, art is actually a substitute for life. It's the reason that somebody once wrote, "Living well is the best revenge."

In the following pages, I invite the reader to join me in reflecting upon the art of teaching and to look at some of the qualities that go into the making of an effective teacher. For the past twenty-one years I've taught English and American history to seventh, eighth, and ninth graders at the New Canaan Country School, a highly regarded independent day school here in Connecticut. I do not pretend, nor would I ever claim, to be a model of perfection inside, let alone outside, of the classroom. But honesty does compel me to mention that over the years I have enjoyed more than my share of successes with many of my students. In addition, I've had the good fortune to include among my colleagues a number of outstanding teachers whose methods in the classroom I have closely observed along the way. One thing is abundantly clear: the most successful teachers have in common many of the same qualities that seem to set them apart from the others.

Now that I've decided to alter the direction, if not the course of my own life, I'd like to leave behind something of value from which others might benefit. If my words can generate a new appreciation for teaching as a creative art, then perhaps they will also enable the reader to see that, in the final analysis, the qualities that make for the most effective teachers are the same as those that make for the most successful human beings. In addition, we can see that the daily lessons of a teacher extend well beyond the boundaries of the four walls of the classroom. There are, indeed, life lessons to be learned for all of us.

By using a conversation between two people, I hope to engage the reader in an exchange of ideas in which the content takes on the feel of a dialogue rather than the tone of a lecture. Naturally, you'll be asked to do your share of the thinking. If we're lucky, we might even have the good fortune along the way to become partners in the process of learning. It seems like a good place to begin.

The Conversation

Every child comes into the world with a zest for life; yet so many adults seem to end up going about their daily activities with a sense of hapless resignation. It almost seems that children and poets and saints are the only ones who are able to hold on to their childlike enthusiasm for living. Does it have to be like this? Isn't there a way that we can encourage our children to carry over some of that creative energy into their adult lives?

Well, Pablo Picasso once said, "Every child is an artist. The problem is how to remain an artist once he grows up." That's so true. I would say that a basic challenge for teachers is to find a way to encourage our children to hold on to the childlike qualities of the creative artist, including curiosity, innocence, and imagination. (By the way, there's a big difference between *childlike* and *childish*.) A Chinese philosopher named Mencius once touched upon the heart of the matter when he said, "The great man is he who has not lost the child's heart." The point is that within every adult beats the heart of a child, but the problem is that over the years we tend to lose touch with the childlike part of our nature. So teachers can play a key role in helping their students to channel their creative energies at the same time that they themselves are holding on to something important in their own lives.

The most successful teachers are those people who continue to see the world through the eyes of a child. They don't ever lose sight of the fact that they once were students, too. It seems that some teachers forget that at one time in their lives the shoe was on the other foot. The same holds true for many other adults as well. Do you remember the feeling of sitting in a classroom all day long? It's not an easy thing to do at any age. (You should try sitting through an afternoon of faculty meetings some time!) Teachers really need to make a special effort to view the world through the eyes of their students. It's so important that they try to get in touch with their own past. In the words of Ralph Waldo Emerson, "There is no teaching until the pupil is brought into the same state or principle in which you are; a transfusion takes place; he is you, and you are he." That's true, but I believe that for the process of learning to really begin to take place, it is the teacher who bears the responsibility for entering into the world of the child rather than the other way around.

* * * * *

You make it sound like teaching is a two-way street. In a sense, the children are doing their part by adding something of real value to the lives of the teachers.

The most successful teachers look upon their students as partners in the process of learning. "The art of teaching is the art of assisting discovery," said Mark Van Doren, the American poet and critic. Of course that presents a whole different way of looking at the idea of authority. It's kind of a reversal of the old order of things. In recent years teachers and their students have begun to view their traditional roles in a new way. In the ideal setting the focus shifts from the authority of the teacher to the needs of the student. "We teachers can only help the work going on, as servants wait upon a master," said Maria Montessori, the Italian educator. That's so true. And the paradox is that the more authority a teacher is willing to share, the more respect he gains from each of his students. In fact, the most effective teachers understand the irony that most of the time we simply need to keep out of the student's way. Cicero, the Roman orator and philosopher, put it more bluntly: "The authority of those who teach is often an obstacle to those who want to learn."

* * * * *

You certainly don't sound like the kind of teacher most of us remember in school. When I look back, the teacher usually ruled the roost with an iron hand. By the end of the year it was mostly, "No more lessons, no more books; no more teachers' dirty looks!"

When I was in boarding school, we referred to our teachers as masters. At the time I never really thought too much about the real meaning of the word. But now sometimes I wonder. Wouldn't that mean that we, as the students, were the slaves? Frankly, in those days that's pretty much the way I felt most of the time about the relationship between the students and the teachers. (By the way, they say that times have changed in my old boarding school. I hope so!)

On Parents' Night I always tell the parents that one of the reasons I became a teacher has its source in my own memories of spending four years in a boarding school. Today I try to instill in my students the same high academic standards, especially in their writing, but I also want to teach them about what it means to be a human being. One time I had a teacher who spent the entire year addressing me by the wrong name. "Do you know the correct answer, *Mr. Poole*?" he would ask. Honestly, that's the only thing I can remember about an entire school year in a course in European history. It's no doubt one of the reasons I start out by making a concerted effort to learn the names of all of my students on the first day of school.

* * * * *

Those sound like some pretty painful memories. That doesn't seem like the best way to motivate students to want to learn, either.

That's true. The impact of words can be a lot more powerful than most people realize. "Sticks and stones might break my bones, but words can never hurt me," parents often tell their children. But the truth is another matter. Because the fact is that words can do a lot more damage than either sticks or stones. Recent studies have proven that children are apt to recover later in life more quickly and more completely from the effects of physical abuse than from the results of emotional damage. In fact, the scars that adults inflict upon their children with their words can last an entire lifetime. That's why teachers play such a crucial role by the way in which they respond to their students every day during class. They can either instill fear, or they can create an environment in which everyone, students and teachers alike, feels free enough to make a mistake. "Children need models rather than critics," wrote Joseph Joubert, the French philosopher.

Above all, students need teachers who use their authority in supportive rather than in destructive ways.

* * * * *

But aren't the real role models for children these days usually found outside of the classroom?

Perhaps. But teachers do serve as role models for their students in many powerful ways. Of course they'll tell you otherwise, but the fact is that young people always take their cues from the adults in their lives. As James Baldwin reminded us, "Children have never been very good at listening to their elders, but they have never failed to imitate them." This is one of those areas in which actions really do speak louder than words. When someone once asked Mahatma Gandhi to put into words his message for the world, he responded simply, "My life is my message." The man who taught the entire world how to turn the other cheek was really speaking for all of us. There's no getting around the fact that people define themselves most distinctly by the way they treat other human beings. Like it or not, teachers are required to set an example every single day by the way that they respond to the needs and the demands of their students. "The influence of a genuine educator lies in what he is rather than in what he says," said Oswald Spengler, the German philosopher of history. It's so true that teachers serve as a model for their students much more effectively by their actions than by their words.

* * * * *

I can see that it's a lot more than just spare the rod and spoil the child. But some people would say that this sounds like the warm and cuddly approach that got our schools into so much trouble in the first place. Isn't it true that learning must also involve a degree of pain and suffering?

There's the old saying, "No pain, no gain." These words represent a popular view held by many people in the field of education. Aristotle spoke for many of them thousands of years ago when he told his pupils, "We cannot learn without pain." No doubt there are many students today who would argue that the ancient Greek sage could have better served countless generations of children had he confined his speculations to the subjects of philosophy and astronomy.

In the same vein, Aristotle also said, "The roots of education are bitter, but the fruit is sweet." The sad part is that most people really do grow up believing in the idea that by its very nature learning has to be a painful process: that if it doesn't hurt, it's not worth learning. Of course, there is a certain amount of discipline and hard work that clearly is required on the part of the child in order to succeed. Students do need to develop the kind of work ethic that will enable them to develop strong study habits, to complete their daily assignments, and to master the basic skills of a subject. But the notion of pain for its own sake is one of the more enduring myths in the field of education. It's the kind of thinking that can do more harm than good for the growth of a child. In fact, sometimes the worst pain that a student may suffer can be the shame that a teacher inflicts upon a child when he or she gives the wrong answer to a question. Of course most of the time it's not deliberate on the part of the adult. But it's certainly a very real feeling for the child.

* * * * *

You seem to be speaking more from the perspective of the child than the adult. Aren't you being a little overly protective? After all, surely there must be some children who are just plain lazy.

The main reason that some students have such a hard time learning is that they're afraid to make a mistake in front of their fellow students: it can lead to the most painful kind of humiliation. There is nothing more embarrassing for a child than to lose face in this way in front of his classmates. In no other area is the role of the teacher more important, either. In fact, the way that we react to the mistakes of our students can make all the difference in the world. How do we as adults use our authority? Do we try to support the growth of the child? Or do our words wither the process of learning on the vine? This provides another of those occasions when a teacher can serve as a real role model.

* * * * *

I'm sure it must be pure torture for some students sitting in class all day afraid to look stupid in front of their classmates.

But it seems these days as though the pressure to perform touches upon so many areas of a young person's life inside and outside the classroom.

Sometimes it seems that teachers and parents alike expect too much from their children. Why else would we constantly be making so many demands upon their time? Lately there's been a lot of talk about children no longer being allowed to behave like children. It's true that young people are growing up much too quickly these days; they're forced to become adults long before they've had a chance to really enjoy their childhood. There has definitely been a loss of innocence in the lives of our children. For one thing, they're more sexually active at an earlier age than in the past. (When did all this talk about oral sex begin, anyway?) Those who profess to be in the know often blame it all on the movies. Or the internet. Or television. They want to believe that the real cause of the problem is something taking place in the outside world. But perhaps the adults are looking for the answers in all the wrong places. Maybe we need to begin by taking a good look at our own reflections in the mirror.

*****

I can see that there's a lot more to teaching than meets the eye. Maybe that's why a friend of mine keeps referring to it as the "impossible profession." It sure goes beyond reading, writing, and arithmetic, doesn't it?

The most effective teachers seem to understand that there are at least two different kinds of intelligence: intellectual and emotional. The former can often lead to success as a student, whereas the latter almost always leads to success as a human being. (Fortunate are those few who are blessed with both kinds of intelligence!) The fact is that the people who end up the happiest in life are often the ones who achieved less than stellar results in the classroom. "The world's great men have not commonly been great scholars, nor its great scholars great men," said Oliver Wendell Holmes, Sr., the American physician, poet, and humorist. In his book entitled *Emotional Intelligence*, Daniel Goleman makes the point that educators and others need to factor in the role that feelings play when it comes to trying to measure a person's true intelligence. We see that the ability to read the emotions of other people actually becomes much more important for achieving success in life than a high IQ or a college degree from Harvard. (Or even Princeton!) Yes, it is satisfying to achieve good grades in school, but it's even more important to keep things in the right perspective. As Henry Welles, longtime headmaster at New Canaan Country School, liked to say, "Character counts more than intellect."

* * * * *

Isn't that the concept of the whole child? When a school places its emphasis on all of the different areas of the child's growth as a human being?

Yes, as teachers we really should be paying attention to the emotional health as well as the academic achievement of each child. Recent tragedies such as Columbine point to the vital importance of integrating a proper balance into our school programs in order to keep things in the right perspective. Students need to know that success in the classroom is only one of the many ways in which we measure the success of a person in life. (That's easy for an adult to say!) But the real challenge for the teacher is to seek out the special gift that each child has to give to the world. The difficult part is that often a student's real gifts are those that lie outside the realm of the classroom in such areas as music, athletics, or art, or perhaps in the social sphere.

The point is that a teacher and a student become instant allies the moment that the teacher tunes into the unique gift of each child because, in so doing, he is recognizing the value of the student as a whole person rather than as one who is narrowly defined by his test results in a particular academic subject. "I may be lousy in math, but I sure do have a beautiful singing voice!" When we pay tribute to the emotional as well as the intellectual intelligence of our students, we as their teachers can better serve their total growth as human beings.

* * * * *

It makes sense that the art of effective teaching includes finding different ways to attend to the growth of the whole child. But I imagine that the focus would still need to remain on the academic growth of the student.

Yes. But the real art of teaching means to instill in the child a love of learning rather than to impart knowledge as an end in itself. Obviously there *are* certain things that every person should know by the time he has completed his formal education. That's what E.D. Hirsch, Jr. was getting at several years ago when he compiled a list of facts that every educated American should know in his book entitled *Cultural Literacy*. For example, studies reveal that a majority of our students are woefully lacking in their basic knowledge of American history. It's a shame, too, because students really need to have a grasp of a basic core of knowledge in a whole series of subjects in order to function successfully in the modern world. That said, however, the primary task for the teacher continues to be to inspire in the child a desire to learn. "If we succeed in giving the love of learning, the learning itself is sure to follow," wrote Sir John Lubbock, a British financier and naturalist.

* * * * *

If a child develops a love for learning, he has been given the tools to learn on his own for the rest of his life. But it seems that too often a light goes out somewhere along the way.

That's why the best teachers are those whose ultimate goal is to arouse the natural curiosity of their students. The truth is that every child comes into the world with a desire to learn. It's the reason, for instance, that they are so easily able to master the complexity of language at a very early age. The fact is that the brain of a child is wired to better absorb certain kinds of information than is the brain of an adult. That's why the teaching of foreign languages is now being introduced in the earlier grades; the sooner the children begin, the quicker they learn. But the sad part is what can happen when the outside world stifles some of those natural tendencies in the child. Parents and teachers need to work together in order to encourage the natural instincts of every child to want to learn. In the words of Anatole France, the French writer, "The whole art of teaching is only the art of awakening the natural curiosity of young minds for the purpose of satisfying it afterwards."

* * * * *

So what happens? Why are children so often turned off along the way when it comes to wanting to learn new things?

There should no longer be any doubt that the roots of education lie in a child's sense of play rather than in the realm of pain and suffering. "Play is often talked about as if it were a relief from serious learning. But for children play is serious learning. Play is really the work of childhood," said Fred Rogers, the famous children's TV host. When they start out in life, all children have a natural love of learning; they are like little sponges soaking up the world around them. That's one of the reasons that the first few years of a person's life are so vitally important for setting the tone for success or failure in later life. Before a child ever sets foot inside a classroom, he has received a message from his parents that will serve as a guide for the rest of his days. The fact is that in their early years children view learning and play as the same activity. Sadly, it's the adults who often see the world in a different light. "It is paradoxical that many educators and parents still differentiate between a time for learning and a time for play without seeing the vital connection between them," said Leo Buscaglia, the writer and educator. Thus, the most effective teachers at any level try to retain for their students a sense of play as part of the process of learning and of living.

* * * * *

You speak of the importance of parents and the messages they send forth before a child even sets foot in a classroom. But aren't parents really the ones most responsible for setting the tone in the first place?

There's no doubt that the most important teachers in life are our parents. The truth is that the education of every child begins in the home, whether we like to admit it or not. An old Jewish saying reminds us, "One mother can achieve more than a hundred teachers." That's not an exaggeration, either. One way or another, parents always set the tone for their children. Their attitudes, spoken or unspoken, provide the most important groundwork for a child's ultimate success or failure in the classroom. Do the parents take an interest in the education of the child? Do they pay attention to the real needs of the child? Do they support the teacher in her efforts to educate the child? There is simply no way of escaping the vital importance of the role that each parent plays in the education of a child.

* * * * *

But it seems that these days there are so many outside forces which lie beyond the control of the parents. What about all those young people whose interest in learning seems to extend no farther than the images on a video screen or the pages of a magazine?

True. But parents who express concern about a child's lack of interest in learning need to take a closer look at some of their own attitudes. Sometimes a mother might say, "My daughter hates to read." In the first place, that in itself is not the end of the world, especially for a teenager in today's society with so many other conflicting interests. After all, there are many people who discover the pleasures of reading later on in life after they become adults. Secondly, parents might need to take a closer look at some of their own priorities in life. Have I made a habit of reading aloud with my child? What are some of the hidden messages I convey as a parent? Do I expect the teacher to bear all of the burden? In other words, parents need to keep in mind the importance of their own role in the education of their children.

* * * * *

It sounds like a subject that can lead to a lot of frustration on both sides. Obviously, teachers and parents need to be working toward the same goals when it comes to a child's education. But it seems to be an area where people too often get caught up in the blame game. Isn't there a way that teachers can start bridging the gap with parents? Let's say, for instance, that there exists the need to address a problem in a child's reading skills.

The first thing is for teachers and parents to be able to sit down together and discuss the needs of the child. That's so important because it gives the teacher a chance to try and make a connection with the parent. When you sit down and look a person in the eye, it becomes possible to begin to build the trust that is necessary in order to bring about the best results. If it's a reading concern, I might confess to a parent that as a child I myself was hardly an avid reader. (I was much more interested in playing baseball with my friends!) By speaking the truth in this way, I can hope to gain their trust as well as their confidence. At some time I might also ask about the reading habits of the parent. Often it turns out that reading has been a low priority for the parents as well as for the child. Of course there are usually valid reasons, too. Often the parents have to put in countless hours at work away from home each day. Or there might be other activities to which they choose to devote much of their time and energy. Or sometimes there might be only one parent trying his or her best to play the role of both mother and father at the same time. These are certainly compelling challenges for any parent in today's busy world. But the point is that whenever teachers meet with the parents of a student, they gain a much better insight into the needs of the whole child.

* * * * *

But don't the parents often see their children in an entirely different light than the teacher? Isn't it almost like two eye witnesses viewing the same event from totally opposite directions?

Well, most parents do have high aspirations for their children. And it's true that many people tend to see their offspring in unrealistic ways. "There must be such a thing as a child with average ability, but you can't find a parent who will admit that it is his child," said Thomas Bailey, the American educator. There may be many reasons, too. Often parents view their children as an extension of themselves. They might equate imperfection in their child with their own feelings of inadequacy as a parent. Or else they might identify so closely with their children that they have a hard time viewing their offspring as separate human beings. That's why a teacher always needs to maintain a delicate balance when having a conference with a parent. "How much does the parent really want to know? How much of the truth will I be able to convey?" Sometimes people don't really want to listen to the truth, especially about the things that are most important in their lives. It's like the time Jack Nicholson screamed out in *A Few Good Men*, "You can't handle the truth!" Parents, as well as teachers, are certainly no exception to the rule, either.

* * * * *

But isn't telling the truth always the best way to go in any walk of life?

Yes, but sometimes the most realistic approach is to tell a person only as much as they really want to hear. It's not a question of being dishonest, either. Or cynical. But sometimes we have to face the facts. I can recall a time recently when the mother of one of my seventh-grade students was telling me about her son's anxieties every morning as he left his mother to go to school. "My child needs to feel certain at all times that he can keep in constant touch with me," she explained in her own anxious manner. After a few moments, I had a much clearer understanding of both the parent and her child. It was obvious that the mother had it backwards: it was actually *she* who felt the need to be in constant touch with her child during the day. In response, there was little I could say. As Louis Armstrong, the great jazz musician, once put it, "There are some people that if they don't know, you can't tell 'em."

* * * * *

It sounds like some of the time parents can actually get in the way of the education of their children. Is it sometimes one of the roles of a teacher to undo the harmful effects that can take place in the home?

Over the years I've learned that the most challenging kids tend to have some of the most difficult parents. In fact, the students who require the most attention from their teachers in school are usually the ones who receive the least attention from their parents at home. That's not meant to be a slap in the face of the parents, either. Louis Johannot, a Swiss headmaster, used humor to make his point when he said, "The only reason I always try to meet and know the parents better is it helps me to forgive the children." Actually, there is an element of truth to his words because the seed does not often fall far from the source.

* * * * *

Earlier you spoke of teachers being partners with their students in the process of learning. Shouldn't we also be talking about a team effort when it comes to teachers and parents working together?

Yes. That's why it's always so worthwhile for teachers and parents to make the effort to sit down and engage in a conversation with each other. Whenever I have a conference with a parent, I always leave with a greater understanding of the strengths and weaknesses of the child. Besides, parents need to feel assured that the teacher is working hard to do what's in the best interest of their child. I'm fortunate in that most of the parents in my school understand that they and the teachers are working together toward the same goal: both the academic and the personal growth of the child. They accept the fact that the education of a child is a joint effort on the part of both the family and the educational institution. (I hate the word *institution* because it reminds me of bricks and mortar!) It's true that the entire process really needs to be a group effort of adults working together to promote what's in the best interest for the development of the whole child.

* * * * *

The way you keep talking about the growth of the child brings to mind the image of planting a flower in a garden. I can picture putting a seed into the soil and then adding all the right ingredients in order to help it grow up to be a healthy plant.

That's a fitting analogy. Henry Welles once said, "Children, like flowers, need time to unfold." The most effective teachers try to nurture the growth of their students in so many ways during the course of a school year. Oscar Wilde once noted, "We teach people how to remember, we never teach them how to grow." Fortunately, that's no longer the case in many schools. The most rewarding part is that teachers get to play an important role in helping to bring about some of these changes. On one level there is the progress that takes place in the area of academics: reading, writing, and arithmetic. In these areas we are able to measure the results of a student's growth over a period of time. For example, the results of the scores on their various daily exercises provide tangible evidence of their mastery of the material in any given subject. But the results are much less tangible in the area of a student's personal growth. How do we quantify the growth of another human being? How can we measure the impact that one person has on somebody else's life? It's obvious that the answers to questions of this nature are difficult to determine. The fact is that there are only two people in the world who ever really know the true extent of a teacher's impact on a child: the student himself and, sometimes, the teacher.

* * * * *

I have to admit there's something almost magical in that thought. There must be a special feeling of intimacy that can exist between teachers and their students, the kind that will last an entire lifetime. But it must be frustrating to know that the rewards are often so elusive in so many ways. I should think that sometimes several years can go by before teachers ever reap the real benefits of their efforts.

It's true. Teachers know all too well that the rewards can sometimes be realized only with the passage of time, sometimes measured in decades rather than in years. "In teaching you cannot see the fruit of a day's work. It is invisible and remains so, maybe for twenty years," wrote Jacques Barzun, the American educator and historian. I can recall many times the appearance on my campus of a former student who had achieved a level of success in life that was seemingly in inverse proportion to the various difficulties he or she may have experienced as a student only a few years earlier. (By the way, that's one of the nice things about teaching at the same school for a number of years; you get to keep in touch with many of your former students.) Or a teacher might hear about a student who has gone on to become highly successful as, say, an independent film maker. But isn't she the girl who never did her homework? Isn't he the boy who could never pay attention during class? This leads to one of the most important lessons I've learned as a teacher: that people of all ages really *are* capable of change. Again, it's just that sometimes teachers have to wait a few years in order to reap the full rewards.

* * * * *

It certainly sounds like the final payoff is well worth the waiting. But I'd like to get back to hearing about the growth that takes place in the child during the actual course of a school year.

One way that teachers can play a major role is by helping their students mature in their ability to reason. In fact, one of the primary aims of the educator should be to teach a child how to think clearly. It's a process that involves learning how to organize one's thoughts in a logical order and being able to present those ideas in a concise and straightforward manner. By the way, it's usually around the seventh grade that children become less concrete and more abstract in their ability to reason. But teachers still need to plant the seeds as early as possible in order to foster the intellectual growth of the child.

One way for an English teacher to measure this kind of growth is to observe the ways in which students respond to the books that they read in class. In fact, the literature can provide the teacher with one of the best ways to gauge the growth of a child during the course of a school year. In addition, the teacher can use the reading as a catalyst to help to actually bring about the growth of his students. During the discussion of a novel, teachers have an opportunity to act as a guide by asking some of the questions that touch upon the most important areas in a person's life.

* * * * *

For example?

William Golding's *Lord of the Flies* is a novel that provides a perfect vehicle for measuring this kind of growth for my eighth graders each year. Throughout the novel the author challenges the reader to consider the answers to the kinds of questions that touch upon the very nature of the human condition. How is it possible for a group of British school boys to end up behaving like a tribe of savages?

Would a group of girls react in a similar manner? Are not all of us, adults and children alike, capable of the same kind of self-destructive behavior under the right set of conditions? When the novel begins, the boys set out to achieve an orderly society in a seemingly ideal world on an island that is free of the intrusion of adults. By the end of the novel, however, these same children have murdered the two boys who are the ones most intent upon helping them to understand the error of their ways.

* * * * *

It sounds like a pretty depressing book for a group of young people to be reading.

It's true that at the end of the novel there is certainly not much evidence to point to as a sign of hope for the future of the human race. If we probe beneath the surface, however, we are able to see that the author is actually trying to convey to the reader a hint of optimism. During the course of our discussion, I will ask questions of my students that point them to two specific examples which can serve as evidence that Golding does indeed intend to offer mankind a final message of redemption. First, which one of the two boys steps forward at the end when the naval officer asks who is the leader? Second, why does the one who steps forward break into shuddering spasms of grief on the very last page of the novel?

By asking the right questions, I hope to point my students in the intended direction. Ralph, the more civilized of the two boys, is the one who asserts his title of leadership only moments before he breaks into deep sobs at the end of the novel. It is Ralph who has come to glimpse the reality of both "the end of innocence and the darkness of man's heart." So amid the ruins the author seems to be offering the reader a glimmer of hope for the survival of the human race. But in order to change, he wants us to realize, the first thing a person must do is to recognize that the real source of the problem lies within, rather than outside, each one of us. As Simon says before his schoolmates beat him to death, mistaking him for a beast, "Maybe it's only *us*."

By the way, if my students prefer to view Golding's final message in a different light, I tell them that they are entitled to their own opinion, provided they can support their argument with the use of specific evidence from the novel. After all, the rescue ship at the end is a naval vessel in a larger war, so a reader might choose to interpret the escape of the boys to a "trim cruiser" as a final image of despair rather than one of hope. Again, my primary objective is to ask the questions in a way that will nurture the growth of my students as rational thinkers as well as thoughtful human beings.

* * * * *

In other words, the questions are really more important than the answers.

Yes. The ability of a teacher to ask the right questions is an art in itself. There are some teachers who lecture for the entire period while the students sit in their seats dutifully transcribing their notes. (Are some teachers getting paid by the number of words?) In this way the focus is more on memorizing rote answers to questions than on reflecting upon the nature of the questions themselves. In the opinion of others, however, the questions are a lot more important than the answers. James Thurber, the humorist, summed it up best when he wrote, "It is better to ask some of the questions than know all of the answers."

* * * * *

Isn't that what Socrates had in mind by asking all of those questions to his students back in the days of ancient Greece?

I'm a great believer in the Socratic method of teaching. That's the one where the teacher answers a question with a question of his own. I discovered this approach quite by accident one day early on in my career when I didn't know the answer to one of my student's questions. "What do *you* think, John?" I asked the young man who had posed the question. After a lively discussion involving the other members of the class, my student, a very articulate ninth grader, was eventually able to formulate the answer to his own question. It was a critically important lesson I learned that day. When you don't know the answer, you should always answer a question with a question of your own.

* * * * *

Are you being serious?

Of course there are other, more important reasons for using the Socratic approach with your students. First, when you as the teacher ask the questions, you make it possible for the members of your class to engage themselves in a dialogue. In so doing, the students become active rather than passive participants in the learning process. The poet W.B. Yeats said, "Education is not the filling of a pail, but the lighting of a fire." While lectures do indeed have a time and a place, it's a series of questions that more often than not results in lighting the fires of a student's imagination.

Second, a teacher's questions can serve as a tool for empowering the students. I often tell them, "The only difference between your brain and mine is that my brain is older than yours." When we allow our pupils to discover the answers for themselves, we are ultimately teaching them the liberating notion of how to teach themselves. "No one can *get* an education, for of necessity education is a continuing process," said Louis L'Amour, the American novelist. When we as teachers provide our students with the right tools, we are helping them lay the foundation for a lifetime of successful learning.

* * * * *

It's true that many people do seem to place their emphasis on knowing all of the answers. But seriously, how should teachers respond when they don't know the answer to a question?

Teachers should always feel free to say, "I don't know." In fact, that can be one of the most liberating responses a teacher can make to a student. In the first place, we live in a time when things are changing very rapidly, including the wealth of information that is available in any given field of study. One of the by-products of the age of technology is that people are provided with too much rather than too little information. As a result, the ability to find and make use of the material is a lot more important than the actual knowledge itself. Even many of the so-called experts are often treading water just to keep up with the most recent advancements in their specific area of learning. At the other end of the spectrum, today's young people are often more skilled and up to date than their teachers in such key areas as computers and technology.

* * * * *

The age of information has certainly brought about a major change in the old order of things.

The best teachers have always known that their students also act as their teachers. When we are willing to be open, we can learn something new from our pupils every day. "The teacher is no longer merely the one who teaches, but one who is himself taught in dialogue with the students, who in turn while being taught also teach," said Paulo Freire, the Brazilian educator. It is certainly true that our students always end up becoming our teachers.

But the paradox is that sometimes it's the most difficult students from whom we learn the most. In fact, the manner in which we react to a child who presents a problem says a lot more about us as people than the way we respond to the ones who always play by the rules. There's no doubt, either, that it takes a conscious effort on the part of the teacher. "What are you trying to teach me? What am I supposed to be learning from you?" These are just two of the questions I try to ask myself during those times when it's necessary to take a deep breath and slowly count to ten. (Remember that the operative word here is *try*!)

* * * * *

That's certainly a way of putting a different slant on things. You mean the art of teaching touches upon the growth of the teacher as well as that of the student?

Yes. Teaching provides the ideal way for an adult to measure his or her own growth as a human being. It's important to remember that learning is a process that involves, at the same time, both the students and their teachers. In a real sense, the classroom is a laboratory in which over a period of time you get to measure your own growth as a person as well as that of your students. "Am I patient enough? How well do I control my temper? Do I become too defensive at times?" These are just a few of the questions that teachers have a chance to ask themselves every single day of the school year.

One of the first things you learn is that young people know how to push all the right buttons. (Or is it the *wrong* buttons?) In fact, students are as quick to expose the weak spots in a teacher's defenses as the Trojans were adept at piercing the heel of Achilles with their arrows. That's just an old English teacher's way of saying that students constantly provide their teachers with grist for the mill for the unfolding of their own personal growth.

* * * * *

Might this be an area in which the literature can play an important role for the teachers as well as the students?

Yes. The books that we read with our students can also serve as a barometer to measure the personal growth of the teacher. When I was a teenager, *Catcher in the Rye* was clearly my favorite book, the first novel I ever read in which I felt that the author was speaking directly to me in my own language. "You're right, Holden!" I wanted to shout. "There *are* too many phonies in the world!" But over time I found myself looking at Holden in an entirely different light. When I reread the novel with my students many years later, the literary character whom I had so admired as a teenager had been transformed into a self-absorbed preppie misfit unable to see beyond his own narcissistic vision of the world. Now all I felt like saying was, "Grow up, Holden! Get a life!" It was obvious that over the years one of us had clearly evolved in our way of looking at the real world.

* * * * *

That sounds like a good reason for a person to reread some of the same books over the course of a lifetime. It's like the before and after, first viewing the world through the eyes of a child and then revisiting it years later from the perspective of an adult.

Teachers need to be willing to take an honest look at themselves. After all, nobody's perfect. For one thing, they need to be truthful about the ways in which they deal with their anger. Do I let it build up until it explodes in a single outburst? Or do I express my feelings of anger as they occur along the way? It's not a question of having to rush out and see a shrink, either. (Although that can be helpful, too!) The point is that the more we know about our own selves, the more insight we are able to provide into the lives of our students in order to assist them in their growth as human beings. Carl Jung, the Swiss psychologist, once said, "If there is anything that we wish to change in the child, we should first examine it and see whether it is something that could better be changed in ourselves."

* * * * *

It does make sense that teachers need to have an insight into their own lives if they hope to be effective in playing a successful role in the lives of their students. But aren't we talking about a special kind of person? In the first place, you have to be willing to admit to yourself that there is a need for improvement. Isn't this an area in which the ego often rears its ugly head?

I often tell my students, "Put your ego aside." One of the things I try to teach them, for example, is that it's okay to make a mistake. In fact, I want them to know that making mistakes is a necessary part of living. We learn so much more from our failures than we do from our successes. "You don't always have to be right," I tell them. It's important for all of us, adults and children alike, to be able to own up to our own mistakes. In fact, that's the place where the process of learning can truly begin.

* * * * *

Is it a kind of unspoken awareness that we're all in the same boat?

It starts in the unwritten contract between a teacher and a student. The number one rule is that in order to achieve a successful outcome, each person will give to the other his or her full attention. There's simply no other way. Sister Evangelist expressed it best when she said, "I have one rule - attention. They give me theirs and I give them mine." These words touch upon the very heart of successful learning, inside as well as outside of the classroom.

* * * * *

That sounds like the ultimate rallying cry for a teacher: "Pay attention!"

An effective teacher needs to know which students are having trouble maintaining their focus at any given moment. Ernest Hemingway once said that a writer needs to have a built-in "shit detector" in order to be a success at his craft. (Today that means knowing when to hit the *delete* button!) Well, I've often thought that a teacher needs to have a built-in *snooze* detector. At any given moment it is necessary for a teacher to be able to tune into the state of mind of each and every one of the students seated in the classroom. I must confess that I've been known to make a high-pitched beeping noise when one or more of my students need some extra help in paying attention to the lesson. That's usually enough to allow the child to regain his focus and to redirect his thoughts back to the lesson at hand. By the way, an effective "snooze detector" would never dream of naming names. The point is not to embarrass the child in front of his peers but simply to allow him to return his attention to the material, and, in the process, to provide the students with a moment of levity in the course of their daily routine.

* * * * *

But aren't there some children who are simply incapable of paying attention during class? Who can't help it because something has gone haywire in the cells of the child's brain?

There is a lot of discussion these days about something called attention deficit disorder. Many people, parents and teachers alike, don't believe that the condition really even exists. They say it's just a fancy label to pin on a child who has a habit of tuning out or is unable to sit still during the lesson. But believe me, there is such a thing as ADD. It's something that goes well beyond the normal experience of a student tuning out on the material during class. Of course, no parents want to admit that their child suffers from this kind of a problem. It's part of the stigma that people still attach to any disorder having to do with the working of the brain. But it's really too bad because the children are the ones who lose out in the long run. If they're fortunate, some of them might find help as adults later on in life, but too often the benefits come too late for those whose condition will do permanent damage to the quality of their lives.

* * * * *

You know, it sounds like a teacher these days needs to have the patience of Job.

Well, it can get very frustrating to have to keep repeating the same things over and over again. But we need to keep in mind that today it's a much different world for children than the one in which we grew up even a few years ago. When they lose interest in an activity, young people are used to switching the channels on their TV or turning up the volume on their Walkman. Or they might spend their free time playing video games after school for hours on end. In any event, teachers these days have to compete with so many other distractions in order to hold the attention of their students. That's the reason it's necessary to try to keep finding creative ways in order to sustain the children's interest. "A good teacher, like a good entertainer, first must hold his audience's attention," wrote Hendrik John Clarke, a poet and an editor.

* * * * *

You make it sound as if a successful teacher has to be a skilled actor. It's almost as if the classroom serves as a stage and the students are the members of the audience.

Yes, these days an effective teacher really does need to have the instincts of an actor in order to hold the attention of his students. Shakespeare had the right idea when he wrote, "All the world's a stage, and all the men and women merely players." I can recall a few years ago when one of my students wrote the following words in my yearbook at the end of the school year: "I recommend that you look into acting for you have much skill in that area." Too late, I thought to myself, but thank you for the kind words. The point is that this student was touching upon a basic truth. There is, indeed, an element of theater in the art of effective teaching.

* * * * *

Does it follow that most teachers are frustrated actors at heart?

Well, you do whatever it takes to hold the attention of your students. Late in the fall one year I had run out of patience with the obvious lack of time and effort that one of my students was investing in his studies each day. The most frustrating part was that the boy, whose name was Charlie, was an extremely gifted young man whose primary distinction as a ninth grader was a complete lack of interest in his academic pursuits. One day out of the blue I found myself doing my best Marlon Brando impression, the one from the famous taxicab scene in *On the Waterfront*. "You don't understand, Charlie, I coulda had class! I coulda been a contenda! You wuz my brotha, Charlie." For the rest of the year, all I ever had to do to redirect my student's attention was to flash a look in his direction and silently mouth in a slightly exaggerated manner the two syllables of his first name. The best part came on the last day of the school year when he signed my yearbook: "Charlie. Your brother."

* * * * *

It sounds like the two of you forged a real bond, almost like the members of a family. I wonder, do you think he ever shared this story with the members of his own family?

It's doubtful. Most teenagers tell their parents as little as possible about their activities during the school day. It's simply the nature of the beast. We all know the old routine where the parent asks, "What did you do in school today?" and the child replies, "Nothing." Actually, it's a perfectly natural way to respond during a time in their lives when young people are just beginning to test the boundaries that separate them from the adult world. They're starting to take the first real steps toward asserting their own independence. (Besides, how much did we want to tell our parents when we were that age?)

Then there are those students who tell their parents only one side of the story. That kind of student can present some serious problems, too. They are the ones who always say it's the teacher's fault whenever they get in trouble or when they do poorly on a test. In recent years there has been a real change in this area, too. When I first began to teach, the parents would almost always take the side of the teacher when their child came home and told his or her side of the story. But parents these days have a tendency to place the blame on the teacher rather than on the child. That's the reason that most teachers can appreciate the words of an English schoolmaster who was addressing a group of parents: "If you promise not to believe everything your child says happens at this school, I'll promise not to believe everything he says happens at home."

* * * * *

It works both ways, doesn't it?

Yes. But there are those times when a teacher really does need to know what's going on in the child's life at home. It's not a question of being intrusive, either. Often it can be a matter of simply having the information and then just keeping it to yourself. For instance, the last thing in the world a child might need to hear would be for a teacher to say, "I'm so sorry to hear about your parents' divorce." But having that knowledge would allow me as a teacher to understand why the student might be having such a difficult time in focusing attention on the material. Then who could really blame the child for tuning out in class?

* * * * *

It's obvious that having good listening skills is a key ingredient for success in the classroom for students and teachers alike.

It's true that the best students are almost always the best listeners. They are the ones who are able to give their full attention to whoever is speaking. You can see it by the intensity of the look in their eyes, too; there's a special kind of awareness that goes hand in hand with the art of effective listening. Of course one of the things that keeps getting in the way is the constant noise that intrudes itself into the lives of our young people. In fact, sometimes it seems like there's a new mantra in the land: "Turn up the volume!" It's not just a question of putting all the blame on today's kids, either.

(Remember the Beatles?) The point is that it's important for teachers to model for their pupils the importance of having good listening skills. Students need to learn to listen to each other as well as to the adults in their lives. It's when we learn how to really listen to each other that the best kind of learning usually takes place.

I once read that being able to give one's full attention to another human being is the highest form of love. It's certainly true that listening has become a lost art. How often do we really focus on the needs of the other person? How carefully do we really listen when somebody else is doing the talking? Again, the art of good listening applies to teachers as well as to their students. In fact, it's even more crucial for a teacher to be able to listen well because he or she is the one who always sets the overall tone in the classroom.

* * * * *

No doubt the world would be a better place if we were all better listeners. But doesn't the art of good listening also require the cultivation of a quiet mind? It seems that many people are terrified at the thought of just being alone listening to their own inner thoughts. Maybe it's one of the reasons that many of us have such a hard time sitting down and quietly reading a book. Isn't reading becoming another one of those lost arts for children and adults alike?

Most of us would agree that reading can be one of the real pleasures in life and that books do provide a marvelous way for people to absorb new sources of information about the world as well as to learn more about themselves. Cicero once said, "A room without books is like a body without a soul." It's true, but the first thing teachers must do is to try to select books that their students are going to want to read in the first place. Too often we bore them half to death by forcing them to read many of the same tired old literary works that years ago evoked the same kind of uninspired response from their own parents. Of course there is a time and a place for young people to be reading the so-called literary classics. But chances are that if children can develop a love for reading early on in life, they will be more willing at a later time to come to regard the classics of literature as companions for a lifetime of learning. That's why a teacher's choice of books that will hold the interest of the child is a vitally important factor in the entire learning process. Of course it's even better when the teacher enjoys reading a book as much as the students.

* * * * *

Can you cite an example from your own experience?

One of the novels my students always love to read is *To Kill a Mockingbird* by Harper Lee. It's one of my own favorites, too. The part I like the best is near the very end when Scout, the narrator, recognizes that the man sitting all alone in the corner of the room is her next-door neighbor, Boo Radley, who has just saved the lives of both Scout and her brother Jem. After a few moments she simply says, "Hey, Boo," the first words she has ever spoken to the man who for so many years has been the subject of vicious rumors and innuendo on the part of his neighbors in a small town in Alabama. The young girl's moment of recognition always makes a powerful impression upon the reader, and every year I look forward to bringing the novel to life by reading aloud to my students the entire scene.

* * * * *

It sounds like we're getting back again to the role of the teacher as a frustrated actor.

Well, one day I was reading this episode to my class when one of my students kept interrupting by asking a series of questions which were unrelated to the passage. For whatever reason, she was the only member of the group who failed to understand that for those few moments their teacher, yours truly, needed complete and utter silence in order to be able to render most effectively the dramatic impact of those final two words. As a result, the words "Hey, Boo" had been completely robbed of their emotional power by the time I got to them. Not surprisingly, the other students were quick to vent their disappointment, in a reasonably good-natured manner, I might add. But what I remember most vividly was the girl's uncontrollable sobbing as she came to understand the nature of her own role in spoiling, however unwittingly, the climactic moment for every other member of the class. Later, several students watched as I tried to ease her pain by putting an arm around her and telling her that it was okay, that anybody could make the same kind of mistake. "Anyway," I said to myself, "there will always be *next* year for me to try, once again, to play the role of the great dramatic actor."

* * * * *

That makes for a powerful lesson in so many ways.

But Boo Radley is only part of the story. The best thing about *To Kill a Mockingbird* is the moral message that the author tries to impart to the reader. Tom Robinson, an African-American, has been brought to trial for allegedly raping a young white woman, and Atticus, the father of Scout and Jem, has been appointed to serve as the lawyer for the defense. Even though Atticus clearly proves Tom's innocence, the Southern jury of white males convicts the crippled black man, who is later brutally shot to death in a final desperate attempt to escape a life sentence in a prison cell. While there may at first appear to be little, if anything, of redeeming moral value in the novel, nothing could be farther from the truth.

Throughout the book, Atticus Finch, the main character, serves as a profile in courage. In his role as a single parent, he has a consistently clear moral message that he teaches his children, for whom he himself serves as the perfect role model. In a scene that takes place some weeks before the start of the trial, Atticus describes their neighbor Mrs. Dubose as an example of real courage because in the final days of her life she has struggled to overcome an addiction to morphine: "Real courage is when you know you're licked before you begin but you begin anyway and you see it through no matter what." Through the words of Atticus, the author is able to convey to the reader one of the most valuable lessons of the novel.

On another level, their father is also describing his own attitude regarding the upcoming Tom Robinson trial, which he knows he can never win in a society whose racist values are reflected in the attitudes of Mrs. Dubose herself. But even in defeat, Atticus earns the deep respect of the entire community, white and black alike, and the reader shares with the characters in the novel the knowledge that a step has been taken in the right direction in the pursuit of racial equality in the courts. During the course of the novel, Atticus is able to put into practice every moral principle that he espouses to his children, which provides the key to his importance as a role model for the reader as well as for the members of his own family and for the entire Southern community in which the novel takes place.

* * * * *

As I recall, the book contains some pretty graphic language. How do you explain to your students when one of the characters uses the word "nigger"?

That's a subject all of us need to take very seriously. In some schools teachers are forbidden to assign a book that makes even a single mention of the n-word. It's true that in Harper Lee's novel several of the characters refer to Atticus as a "nigger-lover" because he defends a black man before a jury in a court of law. *The Adventures of Tom Sawyer*, another book I assign to my seventh graders, also makes use several times of the word "nigger." Every year I worry about the harmful impact that the use of the word might have on my students, especially the African-American children included among the members of my class. Should I even mention the word out loud? Will they think that I am condoning its use? How would I feel if I were sitting in their shoes? In the end, however, I know that every year these two novels provide me with another chance to present some very sensitive material in a way that will allow my students to absorb a valuable message that might enable them to be a little more tolerant of other people as they embark upon the journey of their own lives. The bottom line is that I gratefully accept the challenge of using the literature as a vehicle to help instruct a group of young people to nurture a respect for the differences as well as the similarities that help define us all as human beings.

* * * * *

It sounds like the best novelists are teachers, too, and that their writing can provoke the kind of questions that lie at the heart of every great moral conflict.

Yes. John Steinbeck does much the same thing in *Of Mice and Men*, another novel that I assign to my eighth graders every year. In the deepest sense, Steinbeck's work is a powerful love story about the friendship between two itinerant workers, George and Lennie. In the context of the novel, George's decision in the final scene to fire a bullet into the back of his best friend's head can actually be seen as an act of human kindness.

"But how could you ever kill a person if he was your best friend?" my students invariably ask. In response, I always refer them back to a scene that has taken place earlier in the novel, the one in which a rancher named Candy sits by as one of the other workers fires a bullet into the back of his beloved old dog's head in order to put the decrepit animal out of its misery. When Candy later confides to George, "I wish I'd a shot that dog myself," the students quickly see the connection between the fate of Candy's dog and that of George's best friend. They are able to understand the lesson that the author is trying to impart about the importance in life of accepting personal responsibility for one's actions. In this new light, the students are also able to regard George's final action as a triumph of the human spirit rather than as an act of wanton destruction. In the process, the students come to recognize, too, that John Steinbeck was truly a master of his literary craft.

* * * * *

These are some wonderful novels that you get to read with your students. But I wonder, do you ever get tired of teaching some of the same material year after year?

The most effective teachers never really stop learning. "I was still learning when I taught my last class," said Claude Fuess after teaching at Andover for forty years. In fact, recent studies reveal that people who continue to use their minds in an active way as they grow older are the ones whose memories continue to function the best. That's the reason there has been such an increase in recent years in the number of senior citizens who are enrolling in various courses of study throughout the country. They want to keep exercising their minds as well as their bodies. "Use it or lose it!" as the old saying goes. Aeschylus, the Greek dramatist, expressed the same idea more eloquently when he said, "Learning is ever in the freshness of its youth, even for the old." It's true that we get old only when we stop learning, which is probably the reason some people say that age is mainly a state of mind.

Actually, the best way to learn about a subject is to teach it. "My joy in learning is partly that it enables me to teach," said Seneca, the Roman tutor of Nero. In order to be most effective, teachers really need to relearn the material that they teach in a way that will enable them to view it through the eyes of their students. In return, students at every level keep surprising their teachers with their questions and insights, even when the material under discussion has become second nature to the teacher. That's most likely what the Frenchman Joseph Joubert had in mind when he said, "To teach is to learn twice over." Of course there are those times when a teacher really is learning the material for the first time, but the challenge in the classroom always remains essentially the same. "More important than the curriculum is the question of methods of teaching and the spirit in which the teaching is given," said Bertrand Russell, the British philosopher and social critic. In other words, teachers need to keep finding new ways to inspire in their students the desire to learn, regardless of how many times they have taught the same material.

* * * * *

I imagine that the greatest challenge for a teacher can arise when the subject matter holds little if any interest for the student. Does the study of grammar still rank high on the list of the least inspiring subjects for most students?

For most young people, it's true that there is no subject more deadly than the study of grammar. "It's so *bor-ing*!" they like to say. Frankly, in this area I blame the teachers just as much as the students. The problem stems from the fact that most teachers regard the study of grammar as an end in itself; they get so hung up on things like the exceptions to the rule that they are unable to see the forest through the trees. "Just try to understand the *basics* of the rule!" I often tell my students. It seems to me that students would be better served if their teachers could regard the study of grammar as the means to an end rather than as an end in itself. In my judgment, there are only two reasons that students need to understand the basic rules of grammar and punctuation: one, to become more effective in their speaking habits, and, two, to become more effective in their writing habits.

* * * * *

It does seem so vitally important for our young people to learn how to use the English language correctly. After all, people really do define themselves by the way that they speak. It's almost like a way of leaving your footprints in the sand.

Do you know the number one mistake that most people of all ages make when they speak? It has to do with the misuse of pronouns. Even people who should know better constantly violate the rules concerning the use of pronouns in their daily speaking habits. You hear it all the time from news commentators and other people in positions of authority. They don't set a very good example for our young people, do they? In fact, the next time you answer the telephone, try saying, "This is *he*." Or *she*. I can almost guarantee that there will be a pause on the other end of the line. That's because hearing the correct use of a pronoun these days can cause a lot of people to stop and hold their breath for a moment. The funniest part is that the other person is almost always thinking that *you* are the one who is making the mistake in your use of the language.

* * * * *

Is this the part where the teacher starts to deliver the grammar lesson? I'm beginning to feel a little bit like a member of a captive audience.

Don't worry, I'm not going to give you a lesson on pronouns right now. First, I don't want to risk losing your attention at this stage of the game. There's little doubt in my mind that many of us would part ways the moment I started to explain the difference between the nominative and the objective case, which, by the way, is the key to understanding the correct use of pronouns. Secondly, I believe that grammar is one of those areas in which the only truly effective way to teach is through a direct exchange between a teacher and a student. It's a perfect example of a subject in which teachers need to grab the attention of their students not by the power of their intellect but by the force of their personality. Edward Pulling, the founding headmaster of Millbrook School, said it best when he defined teaching as "the transmission of knowledge through *personality*." In no areas do these words ring more true than in teaching the rules of grammar, punctuation, and writing.

* * * * *

But what about all those dreary exercises that English teachers are always assigning to their students? I'm thinking of all those books that are supposed to instruct people about how to write a decent essay. It seems like there ought to be a better way to go about teaching the entire subject of writing.

Well, I have to admit there was once a time when I myself thought about writing a book entitled *A Handbook for Students Who Hate to Write*. The idea would be to teach students, young and old alike, how to write an effective essay, by, one, including only those rules of grammar and punctuation that would improve their actual writing; two, making use of humorous examples along the way to illustrate each new concept; and, three, giving clear, simple guidelines for writing effective sentences and paragraphs.

I was convinced that a book of this nature could provide help for students at every level. But after a few false starts, I came to understand more fully that it's primarily by the force of one's personality that a teacher is able to hold the attention of his students, especially when they find the subject matter to be less than inspiring in nature. It's another example of the need for teachers and their pupils to have a direct and personal connection in order to bring about the most effective kind of learning in the classroom. It's the reason that the printed word in any form will never be able to take the place of an instructor who is fully engaged in a dialogue with a group of students seated together in a classroom. It's also the reason that it's almost impossible to find a book that can teach a student how to write a successful essay. The truth is that, in most cases, the printed word can only serve as a substitute for the real thing.

* * * * *

I can recall a time when weak reading skills were a cause of major concern in our schools. Now we also keep hearing that students are woefully lacking in their writing skills.

Yes. In this day and age, writing a decent paragraph has become a lost art. That's the reason most colleges require entering students to take a course in basic writing skills during their first year. Only recently, in fact, the authorities announced that in the future the SAT's will include a section on writing skills in which the applicants will have to write an essay on an assigned topic. The college admissions people have obviously recognized the need to evaluate a writing sample that is the work of the student himself rather than a collaborative effort on the part of other people, including family, friends, teachers, and paid consultants. In addition, the students must be able to make their own corrections when it comes to spelling, grammar, and punctuation.

* * * * *

In other words, test takers are required to leave their computers at home.

That touches upon a real frustration I've felt as an English teacher in recent years. The use of computers has proved to be a double-edged sword, especially when it comes to evaluating research papers and writing assignments. On the one hand, the Internet is a marvelous and valuable tool which enables students to gain immediate access to unlimited resources of knowledge and information. In addition, word-processing, with its liberating effect on the writing process, is a vitally important benefit of the new technology in the education of any age group. (As well as in the writing of this book!) On the other hand, computers often make things even more difficult for teachers in that they allow some of the students to give in to the temptations that the Internet affords by virtue of its very nature. Did the student really write this paper on his own? How come she never writes this well during class? Will I have to spend countless hours searching down sources on the Internet? These can be daunting questions for any teacher in this new age of technology.

* * * * *

It sounds like you have some serious reservations about the use of computers, inside and outside of the classroom.

For a long time I resisted the use of technology in the classroom. But I'm gradually coming around. I must confess that I was one of those educators who view the computer as an intrusion upon the role of a teacher. After all, who needs another piece of machinery in the classroom? It's true that teachers who work in the humanities can sometimes be a little defensive in this area; there's the feeling that computers might one day become more important in the classroom than the teachers themselves. In the final analysis, however, we should bear in mind that there will never be a substitute for the human exchange that takes place between a teacher and his students.

Without a doubt the most important element in the process of learning is still the connection that takes place between a student and a teacher. Even Bill Gates, the guru of the modern computer age, himself once said, "Technology is just a tool. In terms of getting the kids together and motivating them, the teacher is the most important." Those are reassuring words for those of us in the teaching profession who sometimes fear that the techies will one day rule the world of academia, if not the entire universe.

* * * * *

It's encouraging to hear that there will always be the need for the personal touch in the classroom. But how much of one's own life does a teacher reveal to his students during the course of the school year? Where do you draw the line?

Of course that varies according to the style of the individual teacher. Obviously, there are no written rules on the subject. Also, there's a big difference between *personal* and *private*. But sometimes I do use my own life as a way to provide a lesson for my students when I think it might be helpful. There are times, for example, when I might make reference to a member of my own family in order to drive home a point.

* * * * *

Such as?

For instance, there's the word *gregarious*. Whenever the word comes up in a vocabulary lesson, I always mention to my students that I have a brother named Greg who is a very outgoing and sociable person, which provides them with an easy way to remember the definition of the word. Then I tell them about the time I ran into one of my former students in a restaurant several years after she had graduated. "How's Greg doing these days?" was one of the first questions she asked. At first I didn't make the connection, which she obviously could tell by the blank expression on my face. "You know, the *gregarious* one," she explained. Honestly, this was the first time I had seen my former student in nearly ten years!

* * * * *

That's priceless.

Then there's my other brother, Steve, who was killed in combat in the war in Vietnam. I must admit that it took me quite a few years before I would ever mention his name in a classroom. Somehow it just didn't seem right to intrude myself into the lives of my students in such a personal way. (I'm sure there were other reasons, too.) But the point is that now I take an entirely different approach. There's a novel we read in the seventh grade called *April Morning* in which a boy named Adam watches as his father is killed in the Battle of Lexington at the beginning of the Revolutionary War. Every year my students become highly animated as they share their own responses to the novel in the discussion that follows the chapter describing the "shot heard round the world." Invariably, we end up delving into those personal feelings that dwell just beneath the surface of a typical seventh grader. *Have you ever been in a war, Mr. Perry? Would you be able to kill another human being? What would it be like to lose a member of your own family like that?* These are the kinds of questions that never fail to engage their curious and questioning minds. But for me there is always a different set of questions to consider. What role do I play in this discussion? Do I remain an observer seated on the sidelines? Or do I share with my students a part of my own personal history?

* * * * *

Which course do you usually follow?

Well, it all depends on the moment, and it varies from year to year. There are times when I maintain my role as the silent observer and other times when I choose to provide a glimpse of my own past for my students, depending on the makeup and the dynamics of the group. If bringing up a sad event in my own life at the right moment can add something of value to the lives of my students, I would be inclined to share with them something as personal as the death of my own brother in a war in a distant land over thirty years ago.

* * * * *

It's the kind of thing they wouldn't learn just by reading in a book, either. Isn't that what educators keep referring to as a "teachable moment"?

Yes. More and more teachers are discovering the value of the "teachable moment." It refers to a brief instant which usually begins when a student asks a question that may or may not have anything to do with the subject at hand.

It's also the kind of question that springs from the natural curiosity and sense of wonder of the child. As a result, the teachable moment very often leads to the most lasting kind of learning. Of course it's a real challenge for the teacher to know how to respond to the child in each new instance. How do I react, for example, if we're studying commas and a child asks how to use a semicolon? Or if we're discussing Lincoln's assassination and somebody wants to know all about the day JFK was shot? Do I follow my lesson plan, or do I answer the question?

This is one of those times when a teacher has to know where to draw the line. Because it's also true that children have a real knack for trying to get the teacher off the subject. If I answer the first question, how do I respond to the next one? If I ignore the student's question, am I showing the proper respect both for the question and for the student who asked it? Again, there's a delicate balance that a teacher needs to maintain between two polar opposites: the demands of the material versus the needs of the child. What's more, there can be a fine line in the classroom between the two opposing forces of order and chaos. And most of the time it can feel like there's no middle ground.

* * * * *

Teaching really does become a kind of balancing act, doesn't it?

In so many ways. One of the first things a teacher learns is that there is always a very fine line between order and chaos. In order to be successful, a teacher must maintain some kind of discipline in the classroom. And sometimes there's truth to the old saying, "If you give an inch, they'll take a mile." The fact is that it's really much easier to rule a classroom with an iron hand than with a gentle heart. In the words of John Locke, the British philosopher, "It is easier for a tutor to command than to teach."

But what's easier for the teacher is not necessarily what's in the best interests of the child. On the one hand, you want to encourage the sense of play that goes hand in hand with successful learning. At the same time, there's also the need to maintain the kind of discipline that is equally important for the final outcome. It's one thing to share a sense of play with your students, but it's an entirely different matter when the chickens rule the roost. That's why there's really no greater challenge for a teacher than trying to maintain a healthy balance in drawing the line between order and chaos. After nearly thirty years, I still struggle every day in an attempt to successfully walk the fine line between these two polarities. (I like to think there's such a thing as organized chaos!)

* * * * *

In many ways the classroom seems almost like a separate little world inhabited by the teachers and their students. But what about life beyond the four walls? Are you also able to convey to the children that there exists a whole other world on the outside?

Yes, it's important for teachers to help their students keep things in the right perspective. We need to remind them at times that there is a real world out there. There are many different ways to deliver the message, too. When teaching a lesson on the correct use of commas, for example, I might write a sentence on the board which makes reference to a child starving to death in a village in Africa. Obviously, that one sentence speaks volumes about the relative importance of the rules of punctuation in the overall scheme of things. For the remainder of the period, however, I'll go about teaching the lesson as if using commas correctly were the single most important subject in the entire universe. But in my heart I know the truth, and, on some level, I want them to know it, too. That's what I mean by trying to keep things in the right perspective.

* * * * *

What about having a sense of humor? Isn't that another way? Young people don't allow their teachers to take themselves too seriously, do they?

There's nothing like a good sense of humor to help teachers maintain a healthy perspective. Of course that's true for people in any walk of life. Why do some of us have to take ourselves so seriously all the time? It's been proven that people who are able to laugh out loud several times each day lead longer and happier lives. It's the reason that some people say that laughter is the best medicine. But the best part is that teachers get the chance to laugh at themselves, which, by the way, touches upon the essence of true humor. The fact is, there's no place for teachers to hide from their students; it's like the emperor standing in front of his subjects without wearing any clothes. Recently I was interrupted in the middle of a lesson on possessive apostrophes when a girl raised her hand and asked, "Mr. Perry, isn't that ketchup you're wearing on your necktie?" What else could I do but share in the laughter? That kind of thing happens all the time.

* * * * *

What else can teachers do to hold the attention of their students?

Good teachers usually come to realize that sometimes less is more. Recent studies have confirmed that the attention span of the average person these days is no longer than eight minutes (which also just happens to be the amount of time between TV commercials). As a result, we all need to own up to the realities of our changing times. That's why it makes sense, for example, for teachers to present the daily material in small doses at a time. One method that can be effective is to vary the material that we present to our students on a daily basis. In an English class, for example, it might be a good idea for the teacher to divide the subject up into three segments of, say, grammar, reading, and vocabulary. By spending less of the time on each section, the students are likely to direct more of their attention to the material at hand.

* * * * *

Do any other tricks of the trade come to mind?

The most effective teachers know how important it is to keep things simple. That seems to be one of the most difficult things for people to be able to do in any walk of life. How many people do you know who are direct and to the point when they speak? Or when they attempt to express their ideas in writing? For some reason people often equate a lack of clarity with high intelligence: the more complex the explanation, they reason, the more brilliant the individual.

Actually, the exact opposite can be true. A primary challenge for any teacher is to present the material in as direct and straightforward a manner as possible. First, the teacher needs to put himself in the shoes of the students. What do they already know? How much are they capable of absorbing? The difficulty is that the answers to these questions vary for every student. Secondly, it's important for a teacher to be able to put his own ego on hold. There's always the temptation for those in a position of authority to try to impress other people with a display of their own expertise. In this area teachers are certainly no exception, either. But this kind of an attitude runs counter to the spirit of learning because it puts the needs of the teacher above the needs of the student. "Keep it simple, stupid!" goes the old adage that holds true today more than ever. The paradox is that it takes a special kind of intelligence to be able to explain complex ideas in a straightforward manner.

* * * * *

Are you referring once again to the emotional kind of intelligence that we spoke about earlier?

Yes. The best teachers understand that the most successful teaching involves an exchange of the heart even more than the intellect. "It is with the heart that one sees rightly; what is essential is invisible to the eye," wrote Antoine de Saint-Exupery in *The Little Prince*. In order to inspire the mind of a student, a teacher must first reach out to make a connection on an emotional level. Otherwise, it can be a fruitless endeavor for both sides. In the words of Horace Mann, the famous educator, "The teacher who is attempting to teach without inspiring the pupil with a desire to learn is hammering on cold iron."

* * * * *

It sounds like the final word is to inspire in the students a love of learning that most often takes place through an exchange of the heart rather than the intellect.

Ah, to inspire! That is what is most essential if a person is to achieve success in the art of teaching. In the original Latin, *inspire* is derived from a word, *spiritus*, which means the breath of a god. It's so true. When they reach out and touch the feelings of a child, teachers are also touching upon something that comes very close to the presence of the divine.

* * * * *

You make it sound almost religious in nature. I can picture in my mind a kind of silent witness that spends the day in the same room with the teacher and his students.

In the words of Henry Brooks Adams, the American historian, "A teacher affects eternity; he can never tell where his influence stops." In this light, the classroom does indeed serve as a kind of beacon in the realm of the eternal, a place where students and their teachers gather together to learn from one another in the freshness of their youth. That's not a bad place to meet, either.

* * * * *

It's a lovely concept. Now I can see that there is a real connection between the art of teaching and the art of living. Can you sum it all up in a few words for us?

You just did; they're really the same thing.

ABOUT THE AUTHOR

Al Perry has experienced life both inside and outside of the classroom. After graduating from Princeton in the nineteen-sixties, he traveled the country selling textbooks to college professors, and followed up with a short stint on Wall Street selling stocks and bonds to his friends. Following the dictates of his heart, Al then entered the field of education, finding a home for the past twenty-one years teaching English and history at the New Canaan Country School in Connecticut. *Life Lessons* is his first book.

Printed in the United States
29000LVS00001B/463-567